W9-CBC-946

FOR THIS I am

Grateful

by ALL OF US

everyday wisdom
PRESS

BELLEVUE, WASHINGTON

© 2004 BY EVERYDAY WISDOM PRESS

ALL RIGHTS RESERVED. NO PART OF THIS BOOK MAY
BE REPRODUCED IN ANY FORM WITHOUT WRITTEN
PERMISSION FROM THE PUBLISHER.

LIBRARY OF CONGRESS CONTROL NUMBER: 2004106137

ISBN: 1-932855-05-X

PRINTED IN CHINA

COVER PHOTOGRAPH: COURTESY OF BILL BATES

DESIGN: KATIE LECLERCQ HACKWORTH
EDITORIAL: ADRIENNE WILEY AND CURTIS KUHN
IMAGE RESEARCH: SHAYNA IAN
PRODUCTION COORDINATION: SHEILA HACKLER

DISTRIBUTED IN NORTH AMERICA BY CHRONICLE BOOKS
85 SECOND STREET
SAN FRANCISCO, CALIFORNIA 94105

10 9 8 7 6 5 4 3 2 1

EVERYDAY WISDOM PRESS
11010 NORTHUP WAY
BELLEVUE, WASHINGTON 98004

WWW.EVERYDAYWISDOM.NET

waking up to a new day
i have never LIVED before.

Jean Myers, 51, Houston, Texas

MY FATHER,
WHO TAUGHT ME THE ALPHABET
AS HE WAS PATIENTLY SPELLING,
"I L-O-V-E Y-O-U."

Roberto Bracamonte, 35, Brooklyn, New York

My parents, who taught me ethics and compassion.
LISA FANCHER, 47, AUSTIN, TEXAS

The way that friendships endure the long silences and separations caused by our hectic lives and fast-paced world.
LAURA ALMSTEAD, 22, STANFORD, CALIFORNIA

A husband who trades restaurant desserts with me when I decide I don't like mine.
ALAINA SMITH, 30, PORTLAND, OREGON

The friend I can talk to when I don't want to talk about it.
SUSAN HELENE CLARISH, 62, YAKIMA, WASHINGTON

Being of the Jewish faith, I had my Bar Mitzvah on my thirteenth birthday. The only gift I still remember was from my Uncle Irving, my mother's only sibling. The gift was a prayer. I now teach Hebrew school and am often invited to Bar Mitzvah ceremonies and receptions. I offer each of my students the same prayer my uncle gave me. Its meaning holds the power of revealing true happiness: "I pray that you have everything in life you want, but more important, I pray you want everything in life you have."

IRWIN LIEBERMAN, 61, SPRING HILL, FLORIDA

Time to be true to myself and appreciate
all there is to my life.
ROBERTA VICTOR, 52, MATOACA, VIRGINIA

Discovering heroes among my everyday
friends.
CAROL McADOO REHME, 51, LOVELAND, COLORADO

Friends and family who believe in me
without wanting anything in return; who
are there for me when the risks I take
don't turn out so well; and who continue
to encourage me to stand up, brush myself
off, and start all over again.
DAWN MERITT, 39, MAPLE VALLEY, WASHINGTON

Flannel pajamas.
MELISSA SCUEREB, 23, FARMINGDALE, NEW YORK

Those tender times and little ways my children remind me of what is truly important: smiles at scoops of cold ice cream on warm tongues; hugs of tiny hands around my tired body; and giggles at a silly bedtime story.

ERIC RADMAN, 44, MERCER ISLAND, WASHINGTON

The way a puppy squints at the sun when his eyes are still full of sleep.

LINDA OPYR, 50, NEW HYDE PARK, NEW YORK

The snow melting and the cherry blossoms beginning to bloom.

STEPHANIE COSTER, 23, KENSINGTON, MARYLAND

The years we spent reading to our kids when they were small, which turned them all into voracious readers.

CINDY DUNN, 44, GRAYSLAKE, ILLINOIS

MY THREE-YEAR-OLD GRAND-
DAUGHTER, MADELYN, WHO
GREETS ME WITH A SMILING FACE
AND ARMS REACHING OUT FOR A
BIG HUG FROM HER BUBBIE.
SHE IS MY HEART
AND THE BREATH I BREATHE.

Janie Logan, 55, Birmingham, Alabama

Two-out doubles in the bottom of the
ninth that lift both a struggling ball club
to victory and the weary hearts of its
enduring fans.
GABRIEL DAY, 28, SEATTLE, WASHINGTON

My grandmother! She taught me the equal
values of a good laugh and a good cry.
JAIME LEDGER, 26, BOSTON, MASSACHUSETTS

Having been adopted by parents so wonderful, I don't care who my biological
parents are.
CAROL COE, 42, BLUE SPRINGS, MISSOURI

The first time my daughter looked into my
eyes and knew I was Mom.
SAGE CARPENTER, 30, MALIBY, WASHINGTON

As an isolated, single, soon-to-be mother with no childcare experience, I was scared to death of harming my baby. When I was visiting my obstetrician, I broke down in tears. She looked up at me and said, "It's good that you're scared. It's good that you understand what your impact will be on this child. I wish I heard more of my patients say this. You understand how important you will be in building this baby into a mature adult. You'll do well." She smiled at me, put her hand on my shoulder, and suddenly I knew I could do it. Whenever I have doubts, I remember her support. It still means everything to me.

Jeanne Heydecker, 42, Aurora, Illinois

Every special moment I shared with my dearest friend of thirty years, who recently died, and what small comfort I was able to provide her and her family while she was ill.
CONNIE POTTER, 44, PORTLAND, OREGON

Every day that I look up after a rain and see a beautiful rainbow. God's promise to all of us is evident in that one perfect arc of color.
EMILEE FONTENOT, 26, HOUSTON, TEXAS

The TV has an off button.
DEANNA J. JONES, 29, HENDERSONVILLE, NORTH CAROLINA

Strawberry shortcake piled high with lots of fresh strawberries and vanilla ice cream.
TISH CABEZAS, 29, CALIFORNIA

SIDEWALK CHALK, WITH WHICH
MY GRANDCHILDREN AND I CAN
DRAW GREAT, BIG, HUGE, AMAZING
THINGS ON MY DRIVEWAY.

Patricia Lorenz, 57, Oak Creek, Wisconsin

Wedding pictures that bring back memories of the best day of my life.

DANA LYNCH, 32, CHICAGO, ILLINOIS

My new Hispanic friends who are giving this Anglo's stomach very mild chiles to start me on my way to appreciating New Mexican treats.

SUZANNE BORCHERS, 54, SOCORRO, NEW MEXICO

My job. I actually kiss the door when I walk through the threshold every day. I was laid off for months, but now I have a boss I love, work that energizes me, and money to pay my bills with enough left over for some fun.

LUCY PAPPAS, 33, AUDUBON, PENNSYLVANIA

I am grateful for my sister. She is a role model for me, and I want to be just like her.

INDIA, 10, LOS ANGELES, CALIFORNIA

My rescued dog, who never stops wagging his tail and doesn't care if I'm having a bad hair day.

KRISTINE LOMBARDI-FRANKEL, 31, MAYWOOD, NEW JERSEY

I know what I am doing here, and I have a lot of work to do.

BARBARA FRIEDMAN, 58, HOUSTON, TEXAS

My job, where I get to do what I've always wanted—reach out and offer hope to a shattered spirit.

JOHN MARTINEZ, 38, SEATTLE, WASHINGTON

The gift of music, which follows me every-
where and carries me through the melody
of life as I glide to its rhythms and relax
in its comfort.

PAULA KIRMAN, 29, EDMONTON, ALBERTA, CANADA

Not wanting what my neighbor has.

MELISA M. FEARN, 34, MURRAY, KENTUCKY

The times when my wife sticks her head in
the door of my office to announce an
updated baseball score, invariably conclud-
ing her play-by-play with the request that
I come downstairs for the final inning. Is
this heaven?

TERRY MUNSON, 38, REDMOND, WASHINGTON

MY PARENTS DECIDED
FORTY-ONE YEARS AGO
TO LEAVE CUBA AND
COME TO THE UNITED
STATES SO MY BROTHER,
SISTER, AND I COULD
LIVE IN A FREE COUNTRY
FULL OF OPPORTUNITIES.

Sandra Martin, 52, Los Angeles, California

I am grateful for the one thing I hate the most: a lifelong, chronic illness that periodically surprises me from the underbrush like a rattlesnake, biting and leaving me to wonder when and if I will recover. I have learned to cherish everyday events—sunrise, birds splashing in their bath, a smile from my husband, a colorful imagination.

MAGGIE STEWART, 56, PRESCOTT, ARIZONA

Pulling up in my driveway after a horrible commute to see my dog's bright, slobbery smile in the window.

JULIE DULLEA, 39, SEATTLE, WASHINGTON

The smell of my twin baby daughters' heads, each distinct and wonderful, fresh and new in her own way.

LISA ROJANY-BUCCIERI, 38, LOS ANGELES, CALIFORNIA

His, mine, and our children who came together as one family, blending and merging, growing and learning to love.
MARY CHANDLER, 53, CONYERS, GEORGIA

I'm beginning to enjoy the fruits of exercising years of patience with my children.
GREG DUNN, 41, ROCKPORT, MASSACHUSETTS

The chance to dance all day, every day.
JENNIFER JONES, 22, BETHESDA, MARYLAND

Sunday mornings, the newspaper, a hot cup of coffee, and time to just be.
SHEILA KAMUDA, 47, KIRKLAND, WASHINGTON

by ALL OF US   25

The stories seniors tell me; through them
I've been able to learn the interesting
things history books leave out.

amy markham, 30, warwick, rhode island

My rubber chicken, which helps keep my
life—and my stress level—in perspective.

patricia lorenz, 57, oak creek, wisconsin

The lessons I finally learned in my garden,
after trying to "get it" for fifty-four years:
If you plant seeds and do not water them,
feed them, or give them sun, they won't
grow; poppy seeds will never yield lavender;
and nothing blossoms before its season.

arlene levine, 54, forest hills, new york

I work on a small cruise ship in Alaska and am grateful that such a beautiful, pristine wilderness still exists in the world. Every time I see a breaching humpback or a magnificent glacier, I wish that everyone on the planet could experience the view from my backyard.

CONNIE POTTER, 44, ALASKA

A mother whose outer beauty pales in comparison to her inner beauty.

JOLENE MUNCH, 26, WASHINGTON,
DISTRICT OF COLUMBIA

The glimmering evening sun dancing across the lake.

BERTIE KEPLEY, 59, DELTA, COLORADO

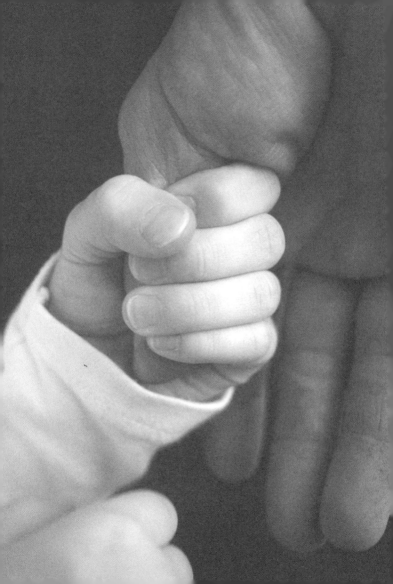

The opportunity to share my father's last Thanksgiving. He had terminal cancer, yet was still very much himself at that time. When he passed away, almost six weeks later, he had deteriorated significantly. That weekend spent with him was the most important of my life. When I said goodbye as I left to fly home to my wife and children, I looked him in the eyes and told him that I loved him very much with as much sincerity and meaning as I had ever mustered. I could see in his eyes that this man of few words loved me equally.

MICHAEL PRICE, 55, HOUSTON, TEXAS

Having the freedom to get in weird, cranky moods and still be loved unconditionally at the end of the day.

Joanna Price, 24, Seattle, Washington

The sound of rain on my windowpane as I fall asleep.

Julie Westbrook, 31, Los Angeles, California

Each and every opportunity I have had to travel. Instead of exploring differences between the peoples of the world, I've been able to see how wonderfully alike we all are.

Sue Johns, 67, Dallas, Oregon

People in my life who make me laugh, and there are a lot of 'em!

Janelle Steinberg, 45, Bellevue, Washington

DOZENS OF EXCITED KIDS
CHASING AFTER FOUL BALLS
AT BASEBALL GAMES;

IT DOESN'T SEEM LIKE SO LONG AGO
THAT I USED TO BE ONE OF THEM.

Rob Bunnell, 30, Eden, North Carolina

Living in a country that protects the rights and freedoms of an individual so I might express my opinions, follow my own spiritual path, and fulfill my creative potential.

JOAN HOLMAN, 52, MINNEAPOLIS, MINNESOTA

Every moment I spend with my two yellow doggies, Casper and Woody. I often try to take in their happy expressions and distinct personalities; I want to make sure that my memories of them are always clear.

KEVIN POOLE, 30, MONTEREY, CALIFORNIA

My fifteen-year-old son still wants me to come to his wrestling matches.

DAWN FARMER, 38, KING, NORTH CAROLINA

Baked macaroni and cheese, with cheese in
every bite!

PAULA GOODMAN, 29, PEORIA, ILLINOIS

The sound of my child's footsteps coming
downstairs for breakfast. That sound is
like music and makes my heart soar every
time I hear it.

ROBIN LIEBERMAN, 39, QUEENS, NEW YORK

The tree frog living in my outside tub who
serenades me to sleep.

AMY CARLSON, 46, LEAVENWORTH, WASHINGTON

My cat, who keeps coming home.

SAM PARK, 47, KIRKLAND, WASHINGTON

The ninety-and-one-half years my mother lived. She was kind, gentle, and so much fun to be with. I was fortunate enough to have fifty-three years of her wonderful influence.

KATHLEEN HAENY, 53, INDIANAPOLIS, INDIANA

Memories of my father.

JUDY MUNIZ, 48, JACKSON HEIGHTS, NEW YORK

God has a sense of humor.

MARY ANN PRICE, 56, HOUSTON, TEXAS

The feeling of accomplishment after a long run in the rain.

CRAIG DOS SANTOS, 20, LOUISVILLE, KENTUCKY

PEOPLE WHO VIEW BOOKS AS SOMETHING MORE THAN COMMODITIES AND DEVOTE TIME AND CARE TO MAKING THEM BOTH BEAUTIFUL AND MEANINGFUL.

Marcia Ian, 51, Metuchen, New Jersey

I was able to raise my family in a country that is but a child itself. Still a work in progress—not perfect, but working toward perfection.

JOANN WEST, 54, GLASSBORO, NEW JERSEY

My partner, with whom I have been able to build a wonderful life, despite the societal myths that demonize people like us.

JOHN MARTINEZ, 38, SEATTLE, WASHINGTON

My dad, who made significant sacrifices so that I might have a better life.

THEMA MARTIN, 34, BROOKLYN, NEW YORK

Grandchildren who think I walk on water born of parents who thought I knew nothing.

SHARON ALEXANDER, 58, OMAHA, NEBRASKA

Vacations with my family, which only grow more precious as I get older.
ANDREW WELLER, 23, ALEXANDRIA, VIRGINIA

Little kisses from babies I don't even know.
JOY HALLMAN, 29, CAMDEN, NEW JERSEY

Unsolicited hugs from my twenty-three-year-old son with an accompanying, "I love you, Mom."
DOROTHY JUDY, 47, NEWHALL, CALIFORNIA

Unexpected smiles.
ERICA BECKER, 37, BELLEVUE, WASHINGTON

Stray cats that adopt me and shower me with purrs that put motorboats to shame.
DANIELLE ACKLEY-MCPHAIL, 32, RICHMOND HILL, NEW YORK

Being able to enjoy my eighty-three-year-old father's quick wit and humor.
CHARLENE LEE, 50, RICHMOND, VIRGINIA

Warm spring days on a cool river, making the first kayak run of the season.
WINSTON WILEY, 55, POTOMAC, MARYLAND

Friends, old and new, and the most amazing friends of all: the members of my family.
ARLENE HESS, 65, VASHON, WASHINGTON

"Stuff," even though I have to keep it all organized and clean. (I appreciate garage sales, too!)
LYNN KOUKAL, 60, BRISTOL, WISCONSIN

When everyone is in bed, fast asleep, safe and dreaming. The house is quiet, and gratitude for the wonder of my family fills me.

SHERRI WAAS SHUNFENTHAL, 45, BURKE, VIRGINIA

The color pink. As a child it was too girly, but now I embrace the strength of femininity.

KAYCEE HOLTON PORTER, 27, SEATTLE, WASHINGTON

The lingering smell of my baby son on my clothes after he has gone to bed.

ASHLEY CANTWELL, 30, BRADENTON, FLORIDA

Legs that can walk, arms that can hug, and eyes that can see the beauty and the struggles of this world around me.

JEAN MYERS, 51, HOUSTON, TEXAS

BEING SINGLE AND FORTY—

AND HAVING A FABULOUS CIRCLE
OF FRIENDS TO SUPPORT ME WHEN
I'M FEELING LESS THAN GRATEFUL
FOR BEING SINGLE AND FORTY.

Amy Eisele, 40, Kansas City, Missouri

The ability to live our lives however we see fit without having to answer to anyone or anything but our own consciences.

DAVE LEDER, 27, HOOD RIVER, OREGON

An atypical mother who has been the most influential person in my life. She has shown me that being a woman shouldn't restrict the choices I make in life and exposed me to faraway places and cultures, the love of reading, and the world of all things creative, always encouraging me to broaden my horizons.

MARGARET BOUNIOL, 44, SEATTLE, WASHINGTON

My parents allowed me the freedom to grow up.

MEREDITH KAMUDA, 22, BROOKLYN, NEW YORK

Ceiling fans that keep me cool on warm spring nights.

BRIAN PARR, 30, AIKEN, SOUTH CAROLINA

Mornings that don't start with an alarm clock.

JULIE HOCKLEY, 41, GREELEY, COLORADO

Young people—their energy and passion reminds me how to believe anything is possible.

SCOTT BOOTS, 38, CHICAGO, ILLINOIS

The way a smile can bring a little sunshine to a rainy day.

SUSAN RIGSBY, 42, ALOHA, OREGON

MY ELDEST SISTER,

who dared me to jump from the highest step in our stairwell, earning me a concussion and a bruised tailbone from the dual points of impact on the ceiling and, subsequently, the floor. She single-handedly taught me three of life's most important lessons: physics, the laws of gravity, and simple common sense.

HEATHER BERRY, 32, BOISE, IDAHO

My mom, who is always willing to listen no matter how small my problem or how many other things she should be doing at the time.

HADLEY MYERS, 21, HOUSTON, TEXAS

The smell of fresh-cut grass.

JULIE WESTBROOK, 31, LOS ANGELES, CALIFORNIA

The color of autumn in New England accented by hot apple pie.

LISA TROY, 37, FARMINGTON, CONNECTICUT

My friends and family. They've offered, in their own ways, to help me through anything, and so far they've done just that!

MARY CULVER, 32, SEATTLE, WASHINGTON

FIRST, a HUSBAND WHO FOUND
TIME TO PUT UP OUR FIRST BIRD-
HOUSE, AND SECOND, THAT WE
HAD OCCUPANTS RIGHT AWAY.

BLUEBIRDS KNOW GOOD WORK.

Kathy Johnson, 59, High Point, North Carolina

The opportunity to live in different countries. This taught me that no matter how different our cultures, we are all just human beings.

SUZANNE CAMPAGNA, 84, WASHINGTON, DISTRICT OF COLUMBIA

My first trip to Paris.

SHEILA KAMUDA, 47, KIRKLAND, WASHINGTON

The sound of my daughter's voice piercing through a crowded airport when she first sees me as I return home from a business trip.

JUANITA ELDER, 45, MARIETTA, GEORGIA

I'll always be a kid at heart—I am grateful for popcorn, candy, and puppies.

DEEMA TAMIMI, 25, SEATTLE, WASHINGTON

When my grandmother became terminally ill she asked my sister and me to take care of her. It was difficult at times, but she brought my sister and me closer than we ever were before. I am grateful for my grandmother's life and death. She was beautiful.

STEPHANIE WIESE, 40, ALOHA, OREGON

The foresight to take the time I don't think I have to spare.

ALEXANDRA WOLFF, 31, JOHNSTOWN, COLORADO

My uncle buying me cherry stone clams from a street vendor in Greenwich Village when I was ten.

CHARLES SLESINGER, 60, SAN FRANCISCO, CALIFORNIA

I am GRATEFUL
FOR JUST BEING me.

Omnissia, 10, Los Angeles, California

The chance to return the loving care and devotion my mother so unselfishly gave me as I grew up.

CAROL OWNBEY, 53, KIRKLAND, WASHINGTON

Being required only to breathe and die. That way everything else is an accomplishment.

DEANNA J. JONES, 29, HENDERSONVILLE, NORTH CAROLINA

The bad times—they make the good ones so much better.

SUSAN RIGSBY, 42, ALOHA, OREGON

The wind on my face and a strong body to carry me through my days.

LISA FORD, 24, KIRKLAND, WASHINGTON

The force we can generate when we unite around a single hope. A few months ago, my husband was seriously ill and wasn't expected to live. That week I began a prayer circle with family and friends. By the end of the week, the doctors could only explain his healing as a medical miracle. My husband, my best friend, put it this way: unity is strength. When there is team-work and collaboration, wonderful things can be achieved.

CAROL MEROLLA, 57, JOHNSTON, RHODE ISLAND

At age seventy I no longer look at my life and think about the things I don't have, but rather feel gratitude for the things, friends, and family I do have.

LARRY NADLER, 70, CLIFTON PARK, NEW YORK

My mother's friendship. As I grew up, she was the chore assigner, meal provider, curfew checker, and laundry boss. Somewhere along the way she become my confidant, biggest fan, wisdom imparter, and, most of all, best friend.

VICTORIA BRAND, 31, MIDDLETOWN, NEW JERSEY

Puppies, pickles, flip-flops, and beautiful beaches.

RACHEL WILEY, 21, DAVIS, CALIFORNIA

THE OPPORTUNITY TO ALWAYS DO
BETTER THE NEXT TIME,
TO LOVE AND BE LOVED,
AND TO LEAVE AN INDELIBLE
MARK ON THE WORLD, NO MATTER
WHAT I CHOOSE TO DO.

Danielle Ackley-McPhail, 32,
Richmond Hill, New York

My best friend, who knows just what to say without saying a word.
SALLY OLINGER, 50, HOFFMAN ESTATES, ILLINOIS

A reckless heart that loves despite its conditioning to do otherwise.
BRIANNA MEWBORN, 22, CLEARWATER, FLORIDA

Dogs that wake you up with cold noses.
KRISTIN PROCTOR, 25, SEATTLE, WASHINGTON

The tolerant, peace-loving people among us. May their numbers grow.
SUZANNE MILLER, 37, DALLAS, TEXAS

Friends who aren't afraid to say, "I love you, and I'm praying for you."
D'JUANA BEASON, 37, BATON ROUGE, LOUISIANA

The man who makes me smile as big as the moon and stars.

ERIN LEWIN, 44, TAFT, CALIFORNIA

We can come to a crossroad in life and make the choice to change directions and see things with a heart full of peace and real joy.

ANGELA KERNS, 46, CULP CREEK, OREGON

My grandmother's hands. They are gnarled with arthritis, but when I look at them I see nothing but beauty. Those swollen fingers still write me letters, dial my number, and make me fudge when I visit.

MARY BECKER, 32, ALBUQUERQUE, NEW MEXICO

I am thankful for my teacher helping my
class with problems we're having.
LAUREL, 10, LOS ANGELES, CALIFORNIA

Having had the good fortune to love
someone deeply. A good marriage is a
miraculous thing.
KATHY WILEY, 61, BETHESDA, MARYLAND

I love my family because I know them so
well; I am grateful that I love them in
spite of knowing them so well.
BETTIE B. YOUNGS, DEL MAR, CALIFORNIA

The sight, sound, and shelter of trees.
MARY KITTLE, 52, BIRMINGHAM, ALABAMA

Friends who will forego an elegant evening at the symphony to sit outside on a summer night enjoying good food, champagne, and conversation by candlelight. To top it off, we kicked off our shoes after dinner and curled up in front of the television to watch a favorite movie and eat ice cream. I kept our unused symphony tickets to remind me of the sweet taste of serendipity.

DONNA WYLAND, 43, POWELL, OHIO

My wife, my direct opposite in so many ways, but also the puzzle piece that contributes to a complete being.
DUSTIN HILL, 24, NORTH LEWISBURG, OHIO

My mother's smile, which can still be seen on her face and not just in a photograph.
DANIELLE ACKLEY-MCPHAIL, 32, RICHMOND HILL, NEW YORK

Feeling confused. I find there are times in my life when I am not sure of much of anything. These are times of real growth. Confusion means all the options are possible. I am open to life. That is a blessing.
CINDY JOHNS, 39, SEATTLE, WASHINGTON

The perspective I gain from every new day and every new experience. The older I get, the better life becomes.

MATTHEW LAURENCE, 35, GLOUCESTER, MASSACHUSETTS

Parents who didn't let go of me until they knew the time was right.

JASON SHIM, 20, MARKHAM, ONTARIO, CANADA

The children I work with. They help me to see the world with hope for a better tomorrow.

JOAN BATTEN, 62, THOMASTON, CONNECTICUT

The written word and endless cups of tea.

BRIANNA MEWBORN, 22, CLEARWATER, FLORIDA

Knowing that forgiveness is life's greatest lesson.

SALLY SUTTON, 52, TORONTO, ONTARIO, CANADA

Birth control pills!

JESSICA BROWNING, 27, HOUSTON, TEXAS

My wonderful mother and daddy-in-law. They gave me the same love that they gave my husband.

GAYLE DAVIS, 53, PINSON, ALABAMA

I am grateful for my legs so I can run track.
I am grateful for my mouth so I can speak.
I am grateful for my ears so I can hear.

ASPEN, 10, LOS ANGELES, CALIFORNIA

The first three minutes after I wake, when I set my focus for the rest of the day. I am grateful for the discovery that if I spend these first three minutes counting my blessings, I notice more things for which to be grateful throughout my day.

GAIL VAN KLEECK, 64, WESTWOOD, MASSACHUSETTS

Rainy, gray days when I can make a cup of tea, snuggle under the covers, and read a good book.

KRISTIN PROCTOR, 25, SEATTLE, WASHINGTON

God shared my girls with me and thought I could raise them without having a nervous breakdown. It's wonderful to know He had that much confidence in me!

SUE HENLEY, 48, COOKEVILLE, TENNESSEE

Having great, lovable parents who have also become dear friends.

SHAYNA IAN, 24, SEATTLE, WASHINGTON

Knowing that the best way to deal with discouragement is to have a grateful heart; it works every time. When things go wrong and life gets hard, I take a look at all the wonderful things I have, and this attitude of gratitude miraculously transforms my world.

JIM MCMULLAN, 65, ISLAND HEIGHTS, NEW JERSEY

Having the opportunity to experience love the way it is meant to be: pure, simple, and honest.

JAMIE MCRAE, 39, OSHAWA, ONTARIO, CANADA

DIET COKE
IN A COFFEE MUG

(IT JUST TASTES BETTER THAT WAY).

Laura Parr, 32, Aiken, South Carolina

My ability to be a saver, not so much of dollars or cents, but of sentiment. Memorabilia, heirlooms, and wishful treasures from my family's past intrigue me, and the love of family shines from them. These special collections reflect what saving is all about.

SUSAN POOLE, 55, CORVALLIS, OREGON

Bacon.

AMY REDMOND, 28, SEATTLE, WASHINGTON

My mother, who taught me how to take care of my father as I was growing up, so I was able to take care of him after she passed away.

MELISA M. FEARN, 34, MURRAY, KENTUCKY

Corned beef hash, corn, and ketchup all mixed together. Don't ask me why, but I have loved this all my life.

ANDY MAYER, 47, WOODINVILLE, WASHINGTON

ALL THE EMBARRASSING,
HUMILIATING MOMENTS IN MY LIFE,

AND LIVING TO BE OLD ENOUGH
TO LAUGH AND SHARE THE
WISDOM I GAINED FROM THOSE
MOMENTS WITH MY CHILDREN.

MARY ANN PRICE, 56, HOUSTON, TEXAS

Having the time to snuggle on the couch with my loved ones to watch the leaves come down in the fall.

SUSAN LENNON, 45, ROCKY HILL, CONNECTICUT

My mother having taught me nobody ever died of a dirty kitchen floor.

SALLY SUTTON, 52, TORONTO, ONTARIO, CANADA

Whenever I argue with one of my children, I try to remember to be grateful for the fact that they have strong voices to speak with and healthy minds with which to form their own opinions.

HEIDE KAMINSKI, 43, TECUMSEH, MICHIGAN

A long marriage filled with trials to make it strong and love to make it good.

MARY BAXTER, 59, MARSING, IDAHO

A husband who understands why I keep
latex paint in a container marked "macaroni
salad" in the refrigerator.

HeLene TuRneR, 51, TaLLaHassee, FLORIDa

All of the stick people, flowers, and crazy
colored pictures taped on my bedroom wall
that say, "You're the Best Auntie in the
whole world."

CLaRa mcnaIR-SmITH, 43, DeTROIT, mICHIGan

Wonderful friends who insisted, after
months of mourning the death of my life-
mate, that I join the living again.

Dee emRY, 37, maRTInSBuRG, IOWa

The awareness to see that often out of life's tragedies come great blessings.
GREG DANN, 41, ROCKPORT, MASSACHUSETTS

Keeping in mind that sooner or later we all get off at the same stop, so what's the rush?
SHIRLEY GREER, 55, BONNE TERRE, MISSOURI

Thanksgiving potluck dinners with mashed potatoes, turkey, pumpkin pie, and wall-to-wall people who aren't afraid to sit on the stairwell to eat.
ELIZABETH KRENIK, 49, LE CENTER, MINNESOTA

A husband who brings me coffee in bed every morning and has for eighteen years!
KIT BENNETT, 40, VANCOUVER, WASHINGTON

BEING ALIVE TO HELP TEND THE GARDEN WHERE MY LITTLE GRANDSONS GROW.

I WAKE MANY MORNINGS TO FIND THEY HAVE CRAWLED INTO MY BED DURING THE NIGHT. WITH SLEEPING KIDS AND DOGS SPRAWLED AROUND ME,

I KNOW I'M BLESSED.

Pamela Patterson, 58, Plano, Texas

The old, great Jimmy Buffett songs my husband and I sing and dance to together.

KRISTA STEPHENSON, 27, SAN DIEGO, CALIFORNIA

Having been laid off from my banking job after fifteen years so I could go back to school and get a Masters in counseling. This has helped me help other people.

ELLEN COSTER, 47, KENSINGTON, MARYLAND

After a serious brush with death a few years ago, I am grateful for every day that dawns and finds me breathing.

FAYE NEWMAN, 59, COOS BAY, OREGON

Waking up to a cat asleep on my back.

SUSAN FARR-FAHNCKE, 37, KAYSVILLE, UTAH

Chivas, the *New York Times* crossword puzzle, and La Bohème.

ROBERT KAMUDA, 59, KIRKLAND, WASHINGTON

The scent of wild honeysuckle in the dark air as I walk among the trees. Though I know that out there, in the world beyond my small woods, more fearsome things lurk, I stretch my arms to the moon, inhaling the safe, damp night.

ARLENE MANDELL, 62, SANTA ROSA, CALIFORNIA

My family and friends. We keep getting better at loving and supporting each other.

MARYHELEN GUNN, 33, GLOUCESTER, MASSACHUSETTS

a son WHO TOLD me,

"mom, Because OF
YOU I WanT TO Be a
FaTHeR One Day!"

Lissa Lee, 46, Covington, Louisiana

The baby birds learning to fly as I sip my coffee before the day's first class.

JASON PRESTON, 20, OLEAN, NEW YORK

Sunshine! Flowers! Gardens! Ocean waves!

AMY ALESIO, 44, SEATTLE, WASHINGTON

A husband who mutes the television and looks expectantly into my eyes when I have something to say.

ALAINA SMITH, 30, PORTLAND, OREGON

The faith that I don't have to take care of everything; God will help.

NANCY FLANNERY-MCNELIS, 44, PORT PROVIDENCE, PENNSYLVANIA

The look on my teenage son's face when he first wakes up. It is half little boy with crazy hair and half young man and something I want to save forever!

SUSAN FARR-FAHNCKE, 37, KAYSVILLE, UTAH

As a child adopted by wonderful parents, I sometimes wonder who my biological parents are. Every birthday I try to imagine them, but as the day passes, I always remember how special it is to be a part of the family that chose me.

MICHAEL CARDILLO, 31, OLD MYSTIC, CONNECTICUT

My beloved cat, who waits to eat her breakfast until we have given thanks together for our food and the new day.

MARTHA POWERS, 62, CAPE COD, MASSACHUSETTS

The smiles on my kids' faces when they rush
to show me the perfect shell they've found
on the beach during summer vacation.

JULIE RANDOLPH, 40, KING OF PRUSSIA, PENNSYLVANIA

Having the courage to remember my blessings before they have forgotten me.

JESSICA MITCHELL, 23, COTTAGE GROVE, OREGON

My infirmity—the degenerative arthritic
knee of an eighty-year old woman, as a doc-
tor told me twenty-five years ago! Why?
Because it's taught me humility and compassion for others. How keenly the pain
reminds me that I am alive!

PATTY MOONEY, 47, SAN DIEGO, CALIFORNIA

FRIENDS

WHO WILL TRAVEL FOR TWO HOURS
JUST TO SEE ME FOR ONE.

Angela Casolaro, 18, Pleasantville, New York

Old friends who cry in cars.

JOSH GORDON, 29, BOSTON, MASSACHUSETTS

The way chocolate engages all my senses:
the jangle of the doorbell at the chocolate
shop, the smell of the candy I see stacked
around me, and the weight of a box of milk
chocolate treats I'll take home with me and
let melt on my tongue.

TINA CZARNOTA, "AGELESS," BOCA RATON, FLORIDA

My children; as I watch them sleep at night,
I am reminded there are still things to
stand up and fight for.

CHRISTINE NIELSEN, 32, LOCKPORT, NEW YORK

That moment of oasis when I am able to let
go and just breathe in the day.

KAREN MOONEY, 52, GERMANTOWN, TENNESSEE

I've been granted the courage and spirit to stay cheerful and pleasant and grateful for the right to keep getting old.

DOROTHY SEROTTA, 81, MIAMI BEACH, FLORIDA

The radiant smile that crosses my lover's face when he sees me for the first time each day.

VIOLETTE CLARK, 48, SURREY, BRITISH COLUMBIA, CANADA

My two sons asking me daily, "Mom, what was your high today?" It reminds me that in every day there is something to be grateful for.

ROBIN MENDOZA, 40, SAN CARLOS, CALIFORNIA

Dreams that allow my deceased son to visit me when I sleep.

JUDITH JONES, 66, FAIRWAY, KANSAS

Little blessings that God sends my way. Just when I least expect it, God smiles down on me with dandelions in the winter, hummingbirds in the springtime, butterflies in the summer, pumpkins in the autumn, and sloppy kisses from my granddaughter all year long.

NANCY GIBBS, 47, CORDELE, GEORGIA

Every decision I have made in my life. Right or wrong, they have brought me to where I am today.

DEBBIE SANCHEZ, 42, NEW WILMINGTON, PENNSYLVANIA

a HUSBAND
WHO AUTOGRAPHS MY LIFE WITH LOVE.

Joan Clayton, 74, Portales, New Mexico

The men and women of America's armed
forces who have served our country selfless-
ly in the name of peace, and the veterans of
every war who have sacrificed so much in
order that democracy may endure.

REVEREND AMY L. SNOW, 53, FRIDLEY, MINNESOTA

The rear-view mirrors on my car. I am
amazed and pleased that I have the ability
to see without turning around.

ANN R. LIGHT, 67, PACIFIC GROVE, CALIFORNIA

Time to live with wonder and curiosity.

ROBERTA VICTOR, 52, MATOACA, VIRGINIA

Every heartbeat that helps me recognize
myself as one living, thrumming instrument
in creation's orchestra—what a song!

ALEXA WINCHELL, 43, WATERLOO, ONTARIO, CANADA

Parents who lived the principles they
wanted me to learn.

ROLPH PALMEN, 60, WOODINVILLE, WASHINGTON

A little orange cat with birth defects. I
saved his life, and he saved mine.

JANE JOHNSTON, 44, COOS BAY, OREGON

A younger sister who as a child was a pest.
Now she is my friend.

HELEN LUECKE, 62, AMARILLO, TEXAS

God's way of being there in even the little
things, such as a thread caught in a
sewing machine. I learn again and again
that He truly cares about even the smallest
details of our lives.

BEV FOWLER, 54, ISSAQUAH, WASHINGTON

The early morning sunlight through my kitchen window.

Jane King, 40, Dubuque, Iowa

Memory.

Lois Greene Stone, Pittsford, New York

The chance to really look at my daughter and see her for the woman she is, not the child I remember. I did a good job raising her, but I never saw that or took credit for any of it until I sat back and respected her as an individual.

Maggie Root, 47, Thomaston, Connecticut

Swimming under a summer sky.

Jenn Gatti, 30, Toronto, Ontario, Canada

I am grateful for my family, my house, and my body because my family loves me, my house keeps me safe at night, and my body keeps my insides in, and it keeps me warm, too.

Victoria, 9, Los Angeles, California

A good book to read late into the night while the rain tap-dances on the roof and the table lamp tosses friendly shadows across the bed.

CAROL McADOO REHME, 51, LOVELAND, COLORADO

Summer fireflies in the Smokey Mountains of Tennessee.

MARY CULVER, 31, SEATTLE, WASHINGTON

My sixteen-year-old son still telling me he loves me as I walk out the door each morning to go to work.

KEVIN HEZEL, 38, BUSHKILL, PENNSYLVANIA

At my age, I am grateful to go down a water-slide and survive.

LYNN KOUKAL, 60, BRISTOL, WISCONSIN

Waking without an alarm clock.

CHERYL CHARMING, 41, GAINESVILLE, FLORIDA

Mia, my eight-month-old daughter, who
squeaks like a frog when she is happy. And
she squeaks a lot!

ANNA JOHNSON, 39, DUVALL, WASHINGTON

Parents who took me cruising Saturday
nights down Hollywood Boulevard in our
'63 Plymouth Fury; Ronnie Spector singing
"Be My Baby"; and Chuck Taylor Converse
high tops.

L. A. OSTERMEYER, 34, TUCSON, ARIZONA

My family, who taught me to love loving.

BETH EDWARDS, 24, MARTINSVILLE, VIRGINIA

FINALLY BEING ABLE
TO LOOK IN THE MIRROR AND
LOVE THAT BEAUTIFUL,
IMPERFECT PERSON LOOKING
BACK AT me.

Paula Goodman, 29, Peoria, Illinois

The freedom to worship God in this country I love, and the Lord's allowing these old eyes to see three great-grandchildren—so far.

RUTH ERICKSON, 70, GREEN BAY, WISCONSIN

The ability to write. While I can't be sure my writing is "good," it is one of the most satisfying ways I have to express myself. For such an outlet, I am grateful.

JENNIFER BERNSTEIN-LEWIS, 28, NOVATO, CALIFORNIA

My maternal grandmother, who taught me all those pearls of wisdom I have made the tenets of my life.

FLORENCE KUTI-GEORGE, 55, BROOKLYN, NEW YORK

My loving, wonderful husband, Louis. He is my prince and my knight in shining armor. Knowing him, I've learned fairy tales do come true.

MICHELE WALLACE CAMPANELLI, 31, PALM BAY, FLORIDA

Roommates who become friends.

CRAIG DOS SANTOS, 20, LOUISVILLE, KENTUCKY

My daughter's first word was not, "No!"

PAT ROUX, 33, SEATTLE, WASHINGTON

My friends. Like the peppers in chili, they spice up my life.

CAROL BOLDEN, 55, CLEVELAND, OHIO

Time spent in my garden.

OLIVIA, 6, SEATTLE, WASHINGTON

In five fast years my husband and I have
had two children, bought and sold two
houses, and moved across the country
twice. We've lost people we love, moved
away from treasured friends, and started
over again when we weren't sure we
wanted to. Our careers have stalled,
stopped, and started again. But we're
still here—together—and our marriage
and love for each other is the one thing
we can count on.

PHILANNE SCULLY, 39, DUVALL, WASHINGTON

My children, who ask for nothing more
from me, really, than my attention.

GAYLE WILLIAMS, 38, GREENBURGH, NEW YORK

a MOTHER WHO KNOWS THAT
THE JOB DOESN'T STOP
AT THE AGE OF EIGHTEEN.

BECAUSE SHE NEVER QUITS,
NEITHER DO I.

Samantha Root, 22, Thomaston, Connecticut

Sno-cones. I can't help but smile when I think of them.

SPROUT HOCHBERG, 33, seattle, washington

All the women before me in this long movement for us all to work, love, fight, breathe, speak, and live—not as the equals of men, but as what we have always wanted to be ourselves.

JULES KENDRICK-LAMB, 20, kensington, maryland

Sharpie markers with perfect points.

LAURA AKERS, 20, sparks, nevada

The resilience I found inside myself when starting out again in life.

ENID PORTNOY, 67, rockville, maryland

I got on the baseball team.

JOEY, 10, CHICAGO, ILLINOIS

I got on the baseball team.

ROBERT KAMUDA, 59, KIRKLAND, WASHINGTON

Grass that needs mowing.

ELIZABETH KRONIK, 42, LE CENTER, MINNESOTA

My sobriety.

JAMES VOKETAITIS, 50, QUEENS, NEW YORK

My best friend, who laughs with me and
cries with me, and has the loving heart to
know when to do which.

BEV FOWLER, 54, ISSAQUAH, WASHINGTON

Microwave mashed potatoes . . . mmm.
ALEXIS, 14, ROCKWOOD, MICHIGAN

My son. He showed me the best things in
life are the ones I am completely unpre-
pared for.
HEIDI GONZALES, 25, NEW ORLEANS, LOUISIANA

A second chance to enjoy life after I was
diagnosed with cancer and had emergency
surgery. When faced with how quickly the
certainty of life can be made uncertain, I
am so grateful to be satisfied just to exist.
MAGGIE ROOT, 47, THOMASTON, CONNECTICUT

My open-mindedness, which allows me to
understand the feelings of others.
ROSA, 16, TELFORD, PENNSYLVANIA

My loving, kind, and funny husband. It
took three times, but I finally got it right!
CINDY ELLIS, 44, POTLATCH, IDAHO

Long coats, crowded sidewalks, and snow
falling on downtown in the winter.
KARI MOSDEN, 26, SEATTLE, WASHINGTON

Sometimes, to overcome loss, you have to
lay your pride and "shoulds" to rest and
accept the kindness extended to you. Only
then will you learn what kindness means.
For this lesson, I am grateful.
LOU REDMOND, 39, CHICAGO, ILLINOIS

My mom. She always knows that it's me
when I call, even if I only say, "Hi."
COURTNEY RICE, 28, CINCINNATI, OHIO

MY CHILDREN, for teaching me the things I didn't learn as a child.

MY PARENTS, for the things I haven't yet learned as an adult.

JIM LARSEN, 43, KIRKLAND, WASHINGTON

Unconditional love, but also unconditional understanding.

Jeanette Price, 28, Lamar, Missouri

My laundry sorter. Three simple cotton bags hanging on a frame make sorting laundry fast and easy and keep me from doing anything less than a full load—which means less time doing laundry. Woohoo!

Barbara Dolan, 40, Oak Park, Illinois

A weakness for saving worms after a summer rain.

Alexandra Wolff, 31, Johnstown, Colorado

I get to eat three meals a day. So many people in the world go hungry every day, and I appreciate that I don't.

Rebecca Constantino, 39, Los Angeles, California

MY WIFE, MICHELE;
GOLF; AND FSU FOOTBALL.
NOTHING IS BETTER THAN THOSE
THREE THINGS IN THAT ORDER.

UNLESS FSU IS IN A BOWL GAME.

Louis V. Campanelli, 34, Palm Bay, Florida

Halloween and having the imagination to still dress in costume as an adult.
JESSICA BROWNING, 27, HOUSTON, TEXAS

Teachers who set good examples for students to emulate.
SUSAN HELENE CLARISH, 62, YAKIMA, WASHINGTON

My son's ear-to-ear grin and his wonderful outlook on life.
SHARON MACKNIGHT, 39, FORT THOMAS, KENTUCKY

My grandpa, who operated on a schedule of his own. When I was young, he would often wake me in the middle of the night and ask, "Do you want to sleep, or do you want to go out for coffee?" I always picked coffee.
JENNY TOMASELLO, 40, CHICAGO, ILLINOIS

MY FATHER STILL TAKES ME TO  BASEBALL GAMES.

Heather Dalgleish, 32, Portland, Oregon

Eyes to see the natural wonders of the earth, ears to hear sweet sounds, a mouth to speak freely, arms to hug, legs to walk, and feet to be tickled.

LORRAINE FRAGA, 22, STOUGHTON, MASSACHUSETTS

Paper and pens and the stories I discover hiding in ink.

GARRY HALLIDAY, 50, GRACEY, KENTUCKY

My friends and family who love, accept, and encourage my authentic self—even when that self is pretty ugly!

LISA FORD, 24, KIRKLAND, WASHINGTON

Down pillows and flannel sheets in January.

JULIE HOCKLEY, 42, GREELEY, COLORADO

Having been asked to sit with my girl-friend while she receives chemotherapy treatments and the opportunity to be silent, supportive, and loving.

VIOLETTE CLARK, 48, SURREY, BRITISH COLUMBIA, CANADA

Remembering to be grateful. Realizing your blessings is a blessing in itself, and it opens the door to as much positivity as you are willing to invite in.

MATTHEW LAURENCE, 35, GLOUCESTER, MASSACHUSETTS

Sizzling words and fresh ideas.

AMY CARLSON, 46, LEAVENWORTH, WASHINGTON

Friends who aren't afraid to ask a favor.

ELIZABETH KRENIK, 49, LE CENTER, MINNESOTA

Feeling the fear associated with a massive thunderstorm—nothing makes me feel more alive.

TARA SHEA, 24, SEATTLE, WASHINGTON

My husband's strong hand to hold as we grow old together.

HELEN LUECKE, 62, AMARILLO, TEXAS

Hot chocolate with double-whipped cream, a good book on a rainy Saturday, the snoring sound my dog makes when she sleeps, and the lovely wrinkles around my husband's eyes when he smiles.

ELLEN BIRKETT MORRIS, 37, LOUISVILLE, KENTUCKY

The strength we find inside ourselves when we dig deeper into the wells of our beings.

ENID PORTNOY, 67, ROCKVILLE, MARYLAND

The kind of faith that has allowed me to understand death as a natural and good part of God's plan for all of life.

BARBARA SMITH, 70+, PHILIPPI, WEST VIRGINIA

The ability to laugh at myself whether I've been hit in the head with a basketball at a pickup game or driven the wrong way on a one-way street. Making a fool of myself keeps life interesting!

ERIN HARDING, 28, MORGAN HILL, CALIFORNIA

The sound of leaves in the wind, laughing at the breeze or perhaps discussing the coming storm.

THOMAS HART, 57, MECHANICSBURG, PENNSYLVANIA

Christmas music that will forever remind me of my childhood.

LAURA AKERS, 20, SPARKS, NEVADA

THE BEAUTY OF MY DEAF
FOUR-YEAR-OLD SON'S
HANDS AND FACE AS HE SIGNS
TO ME WITH ENERGY
AND LOVE FOR LIFE.

Susan Farr-Fahnoko, 37, Kaysville, Utah

Grandpa died when I was seven years old, and Grandma came to live with us. I now had someone sharing my bedroom who spoke very little English, and I spoke no Yiddish. One of us was going to have to learn a new language, and I figured out very soon it had to be me. In no time at all, Grandma and I became fast friends.

Grandma's whole domain was the kitchen. I remember coming home on Fridays, running into the kitchen, and smelling the challah that was baking in the oven—a large one for the family and a small braided one just for me. She would sing as she worked and that was how I learned the Yiddish songs of her childhood.

I am grateful that my Grandma taught me the traditions she brought from the old country, but most of all I am grateful that I learned how to be a warm, loving, and understanding grandma to my own grandchildren.

ROSALIE SILVERMAN, 75, COMMACK, NEW YORK

Being able to show my parents their hard
work and refusal to give up on me paid off.
Charlene Lee, 50, Richmond, Virginia

A front door that doesn't lock behind me
automatically.
Ben Grossblatt, 36, Seattle, Washington

Finding a man who is not threatened or
intimidated by my bluntness.
Tina Orlando, 28, Metuchen, New Jersey

When I arrive to pick up my daughter from
day care, she comes running to me saying,
"Mommy, mommy!" and then embraces me with
a big hug. I know that won't happen much
longer, so I am grateful every time it happens.
Cindy Curren, 35, Carnation, Washington

THE DOCTORS, STAFF, and
modern medicine
THAT ENABLED MY HUSBAND AND
ME TO HAVE OUR DAUGHTER,
THE THOUGHT OF WHOM BRINGS
TEARS TO MY EYES AS I WRITE THIS.

Aviva Wulfsohn, 35, Highland Park, Illinois

The look in my fiancé's eyes when he talks about things that are important to him—including me!

KATHERINE LAWLER, 26, WEBSTER, NEW YORK

My four-year-old nephew, Gary, who is battling cancer and whose courage has touched so many lives.

BERNADETTE WILLIAMS, 32, KISSIMMEE, FLORIDA

My teenage sister who recently came to visit me at college where she exercised her newfound autonomy and maturity all week long. She fell asleep one night while I was typing a paper. Seeing her fast asleep, I saw how young she still was; I saw the baby face she made when I held her in the delivery room. She suddenly looked so delicate.

MICHELLE LAFRANCE, 22, ONEONTA, NEW YORK

My friendships with people both much older and much younger than myself. I learn from their experiences and pass along my own.

PAULA KIRMAN, 29, EDMONTON, ALBERTA, CANADA

Adult children who call and keep me informed of all their activities and frustrations and send me such heartfelt love and concern.

ANN R. LIGHT, 67, PACIFIC GROVE, CALIFORNIA

The mischievous glee with which good poetry awakens my inner mysteries.

GARRY HALLIDAY, 50, GRACEY, KENTUCKY

Feet dangling in the lake.

KARI MOSDEN, 26, SEATTLE, WASHINGTON

Those rare moments when one of my independent teenage daughters looks to me for help, making me feel like I've just won the lottery.

MICHELLE READ, 36, VACAVILLE, CALIFORNIA

Kindness given unrequested, without complaint, and without the expectation that it will be returned.

BETH EDWARDS, 24, MARTINSVILLE, VIRGINIA

My birth control failed! Turned out to be the best thing that ever happened to me, and my daughter (who is now in her twenties) has been the greatest joy of my life.

BETSY PRINGLE, 51, KIRKLAND, WASHINGTON

The Beatles' music as the soundtrack of my life.

MARY KOLADA SCOTT, 51, VENTURA, CALIFORNIA

I have begun to make peace with the
Cosmic Joke; it's always there, and I've
started to remember to laugh—even when
the punch line is me.

MATTHEW LAURENCE, 35, GLOUCESTER, MASSACHUSETTS

Being allowed to rely on my faith regard-
less of what others think or believe.

DAWN MERITT, 39, MAPLE VALLEY, WASHINGTON

The one and only photo I have of my mom.

CLARA MCNAIR-SMITH, 43, DETROIT, MICHIGAN

The ever-changing shadows across the
mountains as the sun begins to set. It's my
favorite time of day.

JEFF DAVIDS, 38, SAN DIEGO, CALIFORNIA

ALL OF THOSE GARDENERS
WHO BURY UGLY BULBS IN THE FALL,
FULL OF FAITH THAT THEIR REWARD IN
THE SPRING WILL BE MAGNIFICENT
TULIPS, DAFFODILS,
AND HYACINTHS.

Arlene Hess, 65, Vashon, Washington

The comfort of a loved one's hand still soft and loving after all the calluses of life.

LYNN KOUKOL, 60, BRISTOL, WISCONSIN

The moments when the world and all self-consciousness fall away and I am dancing by myself in the kitchen, singing some senseless tune.

DEEMA TAMIMI, 25, SEATTLE, WASHINGTON

Each morning's fresh canvas upon which to paint a new picture of my unfolding life.

BEVANNE SINCLAIR, 54, BOULDER, COLORADO

My daughter's birth mother's decision to release her into our loving home, and the courage and wisdom that she showed in making that decision out of love for her newborn child.

JENNIFER RAISCH, 49, TEMECULA, CALIFORNIA

My child's giggle. It turns my anger to
laughter in a moment's time.

SUSAN DIBENEDITTO, 40, SOUTHBURY, CONNECTICUT

Everything my grandma never knew she
taught me.

SAGE CARPENTER, 30, MALTBY, WASHINGTON

Sleeping naked between two velvety blankets.

CHERYL CHARMING, 41, GAINESVILLE, FLORIDA

My five unruly felines who each and every
day educate me on the finer points of life: the
excitement of living for the moment, the
value of being finicky, the joy of a good nap,
the power of the purr, and, last but certainly
not least, that attitude is everything.

HEATHER BERRY, 32, BOISE, IDAHO

Fenway Pahk.

JOSH GORDON, 29, BOSTON, MASSACHUSETTS

My old bicycle, built in 1945, with the
biggest, fattest tires and a seat wide enough
for my own.

PATRICIA LORENZ, 57, OAK CREEK, WISCONSIN

Knowing that although peace might not
exist on a universal level, it can be present
in my home every night. It can happen
within me.

JOLENE MUNCH, 26, WASHINGTON,
DISTRICT OF COLUMBIA

My children, for even when I fail they never
stop looking at me as though I am something great.

JESSICA DEVEREAUX, 28, ARROYO GRANDE, CALIFORNIA

WHEN I LOSE MY GRIP ON LIFE,

 DOESN'T LOSE HIS GRIP ON ME!

Annette Budzban, 48, Wildwood, Illinois

The quiet moments when my son tells me that he loves me just for the heck of it.

TERRY MUNSON, 38, REDMOND, WASHINGTON

Change and choice. Both seem to be constants in my world, but it was only recently that I saw they always walk hand-in-hand. Through careers, growing children, homes, and even a husband once, change was just something to deal with. When some difficult changes came, the concept of choice came clear to me. I now look at change as an opportunity to choose, and choosing love and peace is an opportunity for which I am always grateful.

KAREN COUSSENS, 58, BENZONIA, MICHIGAN

Hearing my ten-month-old nephew laugh so hard he starts to snort!

BROOKE GINN, 19, BELLINGHAM, WASHINGTON

A husband who might not always understand me but always loves me.

THERESA CASPER, 51, WOODWARD, OKLAHOMA

Mixed blessings! I'm often amazed at how
many of the unexpected events in my life
that initially appeared to be negative ended
up with very positive outcomes. Sometimes
we need to wait to unwrap, understand, and
appreciate our gifts of mixed blessings.

JUNE COTNER, 53, POULSBO, WASHINGTON

Still, gray, winter days to reflect and hot,
blue, summer evenings to play.

SUSAN DAY-HOLSINGER, 39, SOUND BEACH, NEW YORK

Friends who take otherwise garbage-bound
black jellybeans off my hands.

JASON SHIM, 20, MARKHAM, ONTARIO, CANADA

My baby's open-mouthed kisses.

Dana Lynch, 32, Chicago, Illinois

A crisp eddy turn behind a mid-river rock.

Winston Wiley, 55, Potomac, Maryland

My support circle of men in recovery from addiction. These are the guys that continuously teach me and enrich my life by sharing their bountiful wisdom, experience, strength, and hope.

John Martinez, 38, Seattle, Washington

Having the ability to forgive, even when I have not forgotten.

Jessica Mitchell, 23, Cottage Grove, Oregon

The lovely written word. When the world is burning itself to ashes, I can always go back ten or one hundred pages, whatever it takes, to get to that last great love scene.

JULES KENDRICK-LAMB, 20, KENSINGTON, MARYLAND

We recently had the honor of hosting our son's garden wedding at our home. I am truly grateful for having experienced what only a wedding can offer: pure joy, a prideful heart, and the renewed love for a child who has become a man.

CHARLENE HASHA, 52, BEND, OREGON

The peace and comfort of having faith.

CAROL COE, 42, BLUE SPRINGS, MISSOURI

MY CHILDREN TAUGHT ME THAT
ALTHOUGH I COULD GIVE THEM LIFE,
I COULD NOT LIVE IT FOR THEM.

Sally Sutton, 52, Toronto, Ontario, Canada

I am grateful to have a parent because
some children don't.

aspen, 10, los angeles, california

My boyfriend's willingness to do the dishes
every night.

adrienne wiley, 22, seattle, washington

Questions from my children that let me
know my opinion still matters.

susie yakowicz, 43, eagan, minnesota

I am pregnant with our first child, and
everything is going along fine so far.
Twenty-one weeks today!

susan combs, 31, meridian, idaho

The even terrain of life that allows me
glimpses of blessings, and also the uneven
terrain, for it is there that I gain wisdom.
BETTY KING, 61, MT. VERNON, ILLINOIS

The Lord let me have a handicapped son
who taught me unconditional love.
JO KITTINGER, 46, HOOVER, ALABAMA

That life-changing book that found me and
addressed all my concerns and worries in
its pages.
MARY HANCOCK, 49, ALPHARETTA, GEORGIA

Having a complete stranger smile at me.
ANTONIO, 15, MERRICK, NEW YORK

Recently I had to put my good friend, a golden retriever named Bonnie, to sleep. Though there is always unbearable sadness in saying goodbye to a four-legged friend, I am thankful to have been touched so deeply by her spirit. She was a gift. An animal, yes, but she taught me so much about being human.

CHRISTOPHER WOODS, 52, HOUSTON, TEXAS

My binky and blanky.

SYDNEY, 3, KIRKLAND, WASHINGTON

My husband, who understands why I can't go to someone's house without flowers.

JULIE KATZ, 36, SEATTLE, WASHINGTON

I don't begrudge those overcast clouds.
In the whole scheme of things,
            they have their place.
And although they deprive me of one of
            my favorite things,
They make me appreciate even more
Waiting for the sun to rise.

GAIL LAWSON WHITE, 48, COSTA MESA, CALIFORNIA

My husband and son, for remembering to put the toilet seat down.

CLARA MCNAIR-SMITH, 43, DETROIT, MICHIGAN

The ability to recognize an opportunity no matter how it has disguised itself.

ALEXANDRA WOLFF, 31, JOHNSTOWN, COLORADO

Being able to sleep in on weekends whether I need to or not.

TIM SCHROEDER, 32, SEATTLE, WASHINGTON

My children, who taught me the true art of juggling ten things at one time!

LYNETTE CARRINGTON, 34, MESA, ARIZONA

The smell of campfire on sweaters and
sleeping bags.

KARI MOSDEN, 27, SEATTLE, WASHINGTON

My wife, who tolerated my retreat from
family life as I finished my Master's.

THOMAS HART, 57, MECHANICSBURG, PENNSYLVANIA

The fall of pure white snow that transforms
my world without a murmur.

ANNETTE ECKART, 50, MEDFORD, NEW YORK

Air conditioning. God bless the person(s)
who invented such glorious technology!

JOLENE MUNCH, 26, WASHINGTON,
DISTRICT OF COLUMBIA

MAKING MY MOTHER MY BEST
FRIEND WHILE I WAS STILL IN
HIGH SCHOOL, NOT KNOWING THAT
CANCER WOULD TAKE HER AWAY
AFTER ONLY FORTY-FOUR YEARS.

I MISS HER STILL.

Susan Noguera, 53, White Lake, Michigan

A second chance at living this oh-so-short life.

BONNIE FITZSIMMONS, 34, HARRISBURG, PENNSYLVANIA

Fireworks on the Fourth of July! They give me a reason to yell, clap, and cheer shamelessly and joyously, like a child at her first parade.

KRISTA STEPHENSON, 27, SAN DIEGO, CALIFORNIA

Any opportunity to share a smile.

JAY DUDEK, 31, SEATTLE, WASHINGTON

Being alive long enough to hear my grand-daughter tell me for the first time, "I love you, Grandma Hart."

ADELINE HART, 51, WANAMASSA, NEW JERSEY

Being exactly where I want to be in my life.

ASHLEY CANTWELL, 30, BRADENTON, FLORIDA

Drips of vanilla ice cream running down my children's chins.

MARY BECKER, 32, ALBUQUERQUE, NEW MEXICO

When I'm playing soccer and I score a goal and all my teammates high-five me.

NOAH, 10, SEATTLE, WASHINGTON

The many different looks my father gave me when I was young: love, joy, respect, pride, admiration, and, sometimes, anger.

SHIRLEY GHOLSON, 39, DUBOIS, PENNSYLVANIA

My childhood girlfriend. Our friendship has endured for more than forty-three years. She knows everything about me, my deepest and darkest secrets, and remains my best friend without faltering, compromising, or judging . . . call us sisters.

JANIE LOGAN, 55, BIRMINGHAM, ALABAMA

Wind-blown laundry drawn from the line, fragrant and folded, bringing the outdoors in.

TRISH KASPAR, 62, SAN MATEO, CALIFORNIA

I have been able to turn my painful experiences into tools to help others.

HEIDE KAMINSKI, 43, TECUMSEH, MICHIGAN

Naptime!

AMY ALESIO, 44, SEATTLE, WASHINGTON

HANDMADE QUILTS AND CROCHETED AFGHANS FROM THE LOVING HANDS OF MY GRANDMOTHERS. FOURTEEN AND NINE YEARS AFTER THEY EACH LEFT THIS EARTH, MY FAMILY IS STILL KEPT WARM BY THEIR CREATIONS.

Cindy Dunn, 44, Grayslake, Illinois

Dr. Pepper over crushed ice. Nothing better!

CAROL COC, 42, BLUE SPRINGS, MISSOURI

My seven-year-old daughter thinks I know
everything even though my wife thinks I
know nothing!

KEVIN HEZEL, 38, BUSHKILL, PENNSYLVANIA

Shopping!

JENN GATTI, 30, TORONTO, ONTARIO, CANADA

All the wise people who have shared their
insights through the ages and those who
have written their words down so I can
benefit from them, too.

JEAN MYERS, 51, HOUSTON, TEXAS

HAVING LEARNED THAT NO MATTER
HOW HARD LIFE MIGHT GET, NO MATTER
HOW GREAT THE PAIN, LIFE CAN STILL
HOLD JOY AND A SMILE CAN BRIGHTEN
UP THE DARKEST DAY.
THERE IS ALWAYS HOPE AND
THERE ARE ALWAYS MIRACLES,
AND THEY HAPPEN EVERY DAY.

Troy Pinkney-Ragsdale, 42, Ossining, New York

Angels who watch over my family day and night.

NANCY GIBBS, 47, CORDELE, GEORGIA

Reading a trashy mystery on the couch with my cat.

JENNIFER JONES, 22, BETHESDA, MARYLAND

Having been given a nurturing spirit. I have enjoyed taking care of virtually every patient that has been under my care—they have taught me to appreciate and embrace life.

SUE HENLEY, 48, COOKEVILLE, TENNESSEE

My longtime friends who know more about me than I know about myself.

GAYLE WILLIAMS, 38, GREENBURGH, NEW YORK

The smell of toasted oregano, sizzling garlic, and caramelizing onions wafting through the house as I create my favorite dinner.

suzanne lafetra, 39, berkeley, california

The nourishment of body, mind, and soul I receive when walking on the beach or in the woods, watching a sunset, gazing at stars, or swimming outdoors.

maryhelen gunn, 33, gloucester, massachusetts

Acorns and the promise they provide.

elaine pondant, 57, daingerfield, texas

The tiny, jewel-toned hummingbirds with propeller wings that visit my feeder as if it was an award-winning restaurant.

kathy johnson, 59, high point, north carolina

Living in a country where I can be anything
I want to be.

L. A. OSTERMEYER, 34, TUCSON, ARIZONA

I was able to say goodbye to my grandmother
the night before she died.

AMY MARKHAM, 30, WARWICK, RHODE ISLAND

Parents who loved me, misunderstood me,
disliked me, nearly disowned me, and then
learned to love me again.

DONNA WYLAND, 43, POWELL, OHIO

The chance to add another day to the
mosaic of my life.

JAMES VOKETAITIS, 50, QUEENS, NEW YORK

I'm grateful to be an American and to be allowed to think for myself. (I plan to be the first female President!)

TIFFanie, 15, winona, minnesota

Doubled-over-out-of-control-gasping-for-air-flat-on-the-floor-panting-like-a-played-out-puppy shared laughter!

alexa winchell, 43, waterloo, ontario, canada

I'm grateful for the remedial reading classes I was able to take and the town library that kept me in books for many hot summers. Imagine not reading my child's first letter to me or understanding the newsy e-mails from friends and relatives.

RHONDA LANE PHILLIPS, 44, BLACKSBURG, VIRGINIA

THOSE CRISP, FALL DAYS
WHEN THE SMELL OF BAKED APPLES
AND CINNAMON FILLS MY KITCHEN.

Susie Yakowicz, 43, Eagan, Minnesota

The adversities of life, for though they might try to deplete me, they also make more of me than I ever dreamed.

BETTY KING, 61, MT. VERNON, ILLINOIS

Days when I wake up in the morning and have no idea what I'll be doing all day long.

HADLEY MYERS, 21, HOUSTON, TEXAS

My children. They try their hardest to make me laugh, their smiles are completely addictive, and they supply me with an overwhelming, unquenchable love.

DUSTIN HILL, 24, NORTH LEWISBURG, OHIO

Rocking my two-year-old son in the evening after he has had a bath—he smells so good.

JULIE HOCKLEY, 42, GREELEY, COLORADO

WAKING ON THOSE SPECIAL MORNINGS
WHEN MY DAUGHTER HAS QUIETLY
SLIPPED INTO MY BEDROOM TO GIVE ME A
GOOD MORNING SNUGGLE
AND THEN FALLEN ASLEEP IN MY ARMS.

Juanita Elder, 45, Marietta, Georgia

Having a teenage son who respects me and isn't afraid to tell me he loves me in front of his friends.

Jamie McRae, 39, Oshawa, Ontario, Canada

Looking in the mirror each morning and liking the person looking back.

Bevanne Sinclair, 54, Boulder, Colorado

Friends who care deeply about me even when I'm not being a particularly good friend in return.

Tara Silca, 24, Seattle, Washington

The first blooms of the season on my rose bushes—they are always the biggest and most fragrant of the year.

Cindy Curren, 35, Carnation, Washington

THE  THAT COMES FROM KNOWING
ANYTHING IS POSSIBLE.

Susan Landon, 57, Somerville, Massachusetts

The soul, which inspires us to chase our
dreams, have faith in what we feel, and
have hope that whatever we do lives long
after we are gone.

JEANETTE PRICE, 28, LAMAR, MISSOURI

My husband, who is convinced that I am
smart and helps me believe it, too.

MERRY BUSH, 57, OLGA, WASHINGTON

I can still see the beauty in a sunrise.

DAWN FARMER, 38, KING, NORTH CAROLINA

My instructor, Michele, who taught me
that inner beauty is the most important
part of a person's appearance.

HEIDI GONZALES, 25, NEW ORLEANS, LOUISIANA

My sixteen-year-old son who recently said, "I don't get why people think a driver's license means freedom! Freedom is in the passenger's seat!"

MARY HANCOCK, 49, ALPHARETTA, GEORGIA

The way Christmas enters my home every year, sneaking in on the branches of a sweet-smelling Douglas fir.

ALAINA SMITH, 30, PORTLAND, OREGON

Songs that narrate my days and serenade my nights.

CAROL MCADOO REHME, 51, LOVELAND, COLORADO

Even if I can no longer touch my toes, I can still see them.

RALPH PALMEN, 60, WOODINVILLE, WASHINGTON

My husband's deathly cold feet stealing warmth from my own at night.

LISA ROJANY-BUCCIERI, 38, LOS ANGELES, CALIFORNIA

I am quite old, and I am very happy to have lived through an era of extraordinary technological development. I will never forget how thrilled I was the day men landed on the moon—since then, I have never looked at the world in the same way.

SUZANNE CAMPAGNA, 84, WASHINGTON, DC

The smile in my son's eyes when life really touches him.

STEPHANIE WIESE, 40, ALOHA, OREGON

Love stories, both real and imagined.

MELISSA SCUEREB, 23, FARMINGDALE, NEW YORK

eVeRY OPPORTUNITY,
no maTTeR HOW small,
TO make a DIFFeReNCe
IN THe WORLD.

Gloria Wildeman, 51, Seattle, Washington

WHαT αRE YOU GRαTEFUL FOR?

_____

_____

_____

_____

_____

_____

_____

_____

_____

_____

_____

_____

_____

_____

_____

WHAT ARE YOU GRATEFUL FOR?

_____

_____

_____

_____

_____

_____

_____

_____

_____

_____

_____

_____

_____

_____

_____

WHAT ARE YOU GRATEFUL FOR?

_____

_____

_____

_____

_____

_____

_____

_____

_____

_____

_____

_____

_____

_____

AUTHOR INDEX